OTHER BOOKS BY NORMAN FINKELSTEIN

Poetry
The Objects in Your Life
Restless Messengers
Track (Volume 1)
Columns: Track, Volume 2
Powers: Track, Volume 3
Passing Over
Scribe
Inside the Ghost Factory
Track (Complete)
The Ratio of Reason to Magic: New & Selected Poems
From the Files of the Immanent Foundation
In a Broken Star
Thirty-Six / Two Lives - with Trizah Goldenberg

Criticism
The Utopian Moment in Contemporary American Poetry
The Ritual of New Creation: Jewish Tradition and Contemporary
Literature
Not One of Them in Place: Modern Poetry and Jewish American Identity
Lyrical Interference: Essays on Poetics
On Mount Vision: Forms of the Sacred in Contemporary American
Poetry
Like a Dark Rabbi: Modern Poetry and the Jewish Literary Imagination
To Go Into the Words

As Editor
Harvey Shapiro, *A Momentary Glory: Last Poems*

FURTHER
ADVENTURES

NORMAN FINKELSTEIN

DOS MADRES

2023

DOS MADRES PRESS INC.
P.O. Box 294, Loveland, Ohio 45140
www.dosmadres.com   editor@dosmadres.com

Dos Madres is dedicated to the belief that the small press is essential to the vitality of contemporary literature as a carrier of the new voice, as well as the older, sometimes forgotten voices of the past. And in an ever more virtual world, to the creation of fine books pleasing to the eye and hand.

Dos Madres is named in honor of Vera Murphy and Libbie Hughes, the "Dos Madres" whose contributions have made this press possible.

Dos Madres Press, Inc. is an Ohio Not For Profit Corporation and a 501 (c) (3) qualified public charity. Contributions are tax deductible.

Executive Editor: Robert J. Murphy

Illustration & Book Design: Elizabeth H. Murphy
www.illusionstudios.net

Typeset in Adobe Garamond Pro & Charlemagne
ISBN 978-1-953252-82-1
Library of Congress Control Number: 2023938564

First Edition

ACKNOWLEDGEMENTS

The author wishes to acknowledge the editors of the following journals, where sections of this book first appeared:

The Fortnightly Review: The Lessons of Augustus Sprechenbaum 1-5

Colorado Review: "So the child"

Interim: "Pascal sent forth"

"Each little figure" originally appeared in *In a Broken Star* (Dos Madres Press, 2021) as "The Guide."

Many friends have stood by me as this work came into being, and I am deeply grateful to them all. Two have stood by the poems as well as their author, welcoming them with open arms. The poems extend their love and thanks to Donald Revell and Mark Scroggins.

TABLE OF CONTENTS

PROLOGUE

"The Arch-Mage of Nonsense" 1

"The childhood tales" 3

"And what if all those philosophers" 4

PART I

The Lessons of Augustus Sprechenbaum. 7

PART II

"The accountant is nodding off" 19

"Each little figure". 20

"So the child" 22

"The mind/body problem" 28

"Pascal sent forth" 29

"Behind every poem". 35

PART III

" לייִקע אַ קאָססאַקט אָן אַ גוּמאַם". 43

"The *Zohar* floats" 44

"It's eggs, lox, and onions". 45

"There are places we can go" 46

"Shabtai and Milton". 47

"And the piper" 48

"And in the pit was a chuppah". 49

"You can call it the Plateau of Leng" 50

"Cloak as cocoon" 51

"The think tanks and policy wonks" 57

PART IV

"The cranes soar" 61

"*The most elegant patterns*" 62

"A brouhaha in Mahwah" 63

"The author claims" 69

"At the last station" 70

"The spirit fled" 71

EPILOGUE

"Do you remember" 75

"And the lost ones" 78

Afterword 83

About the Author 89

FURTHER
ADVENTURES

PROLOGUE

The Arch-Mage of Nonsense
is at work in his study
shaping an ego
out of old books of poems
bits of gossip
found on the internet
and vague memories
that were once his own.

The ego is dispersed
across page after page
decanted stuff
from alembics and test tubes
and vacuum chambers
retrieved from space stations
long abandoned
orbiting the moon.

Like a comic book born
of ennui and sorrow
pain and irony
and impossible magic
the ego and its dreamwork
are laid out in poems
panel next to panel
demanding interpretation.

Panel next to panel
in their inane contiguity
defying continuity
yet insisting upon narration
the ego in pieces

like Adam Kadmon
and the laughter of the Arch-Mage
echoing through space.

The childhood tales, the adolescent
fantasies, the studies of the young scholar
alone in the carrel, the I and the interrogation
of the I: it is a journey to a Place that will not
recede, but is out of sight from time to time.
And whether that Place is a displacement,
the exchange of one Place for another,
he neither knows nor cares. *Ko amar Adonai:*
weave a circle round him thrice. Ancient
methods he seems to have always known.

He appears almost to be loitering, as if
in anticipation of someone or something
portentous, when the guide pulls up and
drives him away. From Place to Place!
Psalms, prophecies, chants, invocations:
why did they choose him to be the narrator?
The Voices will not say. He sees himself
at a table, writing a theory of tables,
a song of tables turned into story of tables,
unaccountable but impossible to abandon.

At first he cannot tell one from
another, and he is never really sure if they
introduce themselves to him by name,
or if it is he who names them. Titles
become speech acts, speech acts become
episodes, episodes add up to adventures.
There are rituals and ceremonies, love
affairs and betrayals, intelligence and
counter-intelligence. At that table in the
library, he writes it down as best he can.

"And what if all those philosophers are wrong,
and each poem is a chapter in a Grand Narrative?"
The cat runs his tongue along his leg, looks up
and blinks. How did I get back in the zone?
"Let's call it the Blank Lodge," he says;
"we'll do without the red curtains. As for
the strange voices, you can provide your own."

"And what if all those novelists are wrong,
and the prophet who insists that modernity
is a myth is kin to the Bateleur in the Major
Arcana, androgynous, moving between
the stories, unmaking them all?" The cat
settles himself on the cushion. "Let's
call it Sprechenbaum's Dream," he says.

"And as for the poets, what if they're wrong
too? It's not as if they know what they're
doing. You better make yourself comfortable,"
he says. "You're going to be here for quite
a while. The Foundation has a few more
questions for you." I straighten my tie, look him
calmly in the eye. "I am the Foundation," I say.

homage to David Lynch

The Lessons of Augustus Sprechenbaum

for Donald Revell

1.

It is always rising, even when it appears to be
falling. The spirit, I mean. Agrippa speaks of three
worlds, the elemental, the celestial, and the intellectual.
But I remember the advice of the priestess. Augustus,
she said to me, always remember there is one great
House. Decans, ogdoads, angelic orders, lists of
demonic names. Synods, symposia, conventions:
the learned Hebrew doctors, the Greek philosophers,
the Egyptian wardens of the temples, and all
the stargazers and makers of images delude themselves
or catch a rare glimpse of truth only insofar as they
keep this in mind. "An old man sitting on a high throne
or on a dragon, with a hood of dark linen on his head,
holding a sickle or a fish." "A young Venus holding
apples and flowers, dressed in white and yellow."
Pretty pictures to decorate a palace or a book.
Should a religious reform put more magic into the faith,
or take the magic out of it? Does science oppose belief,
or does belief subsume it? Some illnesses can be cured
by restoring balance to the humors, but some illnesses
are the result of such a balance. The body, I mean.
The body politic. Not Athens, no, and not Jerusalem.
Alexandria.

2.

A visit to the Sphinx, or a consultation
with the Sphinx. Shadowy figures with
the heads of beasts—jackals, stags,
crocodiles. A meal of lamb stewed with
lentils and herbs, or baked fish with
little cakes of millet. Honey and salt,
mint and citron. Then sleep, but not
overlong. A bath, followed by various oils
upon various parts of the body. All this
to say that life goes on despite dire
predictions, heard or overheard, read
in a letter or cried in the square. News
reaches my consulting room across the miles
and decades. The possessed, the soul sick,
the neurasthenic—how long ago was it
that I set up shop, how many times was I
forced to flee, so that exile became my
modus vivendi. And so I let them wander,
refraining from spells and exorcisms.
Let the demons speak for themselves until,
as you hold them, they exhaust themselves
and disappear. But the archons are closing in,
or so Wanderlust reports. My purring familiar,
so cozy there on the rug. I hate to disturb you,
but it's time we hit the road.

3.

Why is the alchemist always depicted
as an old man in a dusty basement?
I was young in Prague's winding streets,
spending more time in taverns than laboratories,
more time with barmaids than alembics and scales.
I watched the elemental spirits come and go,
and stared into the mirror of time. The automata perched
on the astronomical clock mocked me as I staggered home.
In Prague they drink more beer than in Berlin.
Even the rabbis were known to imbibe—you don't
bring clay to life stone sober, however holy
you think the work may be. I can't begin to tell you
how strange those prayers and spells can sound.
What we have lost in dignity we have gained in power.
I have drawn a circle around these operations,
and only the initiates may enter in. By Magia we use
the chain linking earth to heaven, and by Cabala we use
the celestial chain through the angels to the divine Name.
Who made this? *HaShem*. And who made this? *HaShem*.
She sent me the tale in a letter, a commentary upon
a commentary. And so I learned that the letters reached
toward the super-celestial spheres, to capture the power
of the stars. But Pico and his lover were poisoned,
and Bruno was burned at the stake. The apostles
process upon the hour, and Death rings the bell.

4.

Currents and counter-currents, memories and
counter-memories, lives and counter-lives.
Time streams through me, as I stream through
time. Lost among the years, I would find myself
in another city, another circle, another cabal.
At some point, I began to wonder what else
I could possibly be taught. I lost my voice when
I started hearing voices. I have regained it,
but use it sparingly, though at times I have
plenty to say. A patron is a wonderful thing,
and men in high places may offer protection—
for a while. Once the book is in print, there's no
denying it. You've set yourself up, or you've
been set up. It was in the fatidic year 14__,
or was it 19__? We were arguing about astrology
again, or was it telepathy? Time streams through me,
as I stream through time.

5.

Sigillus Sigillorum. Seal of Seals. Not Solomon's,
but Bruno's. Or perhaps Symbol of Symbols,
Signature of Signatures. How do we bind all things
in Creation? Four Ruling Principles: Love, Art,
Mathematics, and Magic. Love the great daemon,
divine furor, tending us toward the Infinite Archetype,
ceaseless source of all ideas.
                              But enough for now!
These books you wish me to translate: have you
considered that they are not yet written? This is not
an insurmountable problem, but at what point
is time to be taken into account? For into account
it must be taken, if these operations, these contractions,
are to achieve success. Enter into solitude, contemplate
the invisible places, allow yourself to be taken
by fervent desire, deny the body's appetites,
and immerse yourself completely in speculation.
Then you may consider the work at hand, neither
ascending nor descending, but spreading from a point
across the temporal horizon. Where have you been,
Stranger? To what powers do you lay claim, but above
all else, who do you love?

6.

There comes a time when one must put aside
all of one's learning. She is said to effect
extraordinary cures now that she has ceased
her studies, while writing a book of her own.
I am not advising you to follow her example,
but there is something to be said for village
magic, side-street conjurors, clandestine
operations on moonlit nights, apothecaries
conducting experiments after shuttering
their shops. Have you exhausted the wisdom
found in these books, or are you exhausted?
What leads you to believe that you practice
a high art? I pose these questions to myself
repeatedly, but only up to a point. They lay
the instruments before you, though they may
not wear the robes and hoods. Be careful,
but do not fear. All of the statues speak,
all of them attest to the power of the gods,
all of them are contrivances, and all of them
lead us to the truth. This much I know.
There were places where I was received
graciously, but none of them felt like home.

7.

Homesick, yes, for a place I've never seen
—no, not even in dreams. The censor sees
to that. An estate, or perhaps only a cottage
on an estate. Often I would prescribe
a rest cure, a sanitorium in a mountain valley.
Sometimes they would show improvement,
sometimes not. Sometimes they would return
with the same complaints, sometimes I would
never see them again. This compound accounts
for a great many of the changes. Alchemy,
or rather its soulless equivalent. I've closed
my practice, well, except for a select few.

One day there is a knock on your door. A stranger
stands before you. I've come to take you back,
he tells you. Is it too late? Thirty seals and thirty
shadows, thirty links to thirty daemons, that which
is unfigurable and that which may be figured.
Inside or outside, above or below? It no longer
matters. But this much I still believe: there are
four furors which may possess us; I have seen them
time and again. Poetry, religion, prophecy and love:
through each we consort with the daemons of the planets
and of the elements; through each we may be restored.
Not a homecoming, but knowledge of the way home.

8.

You ask about my time at the Foundation.
Everything that came before prepared me,
and nothing did. That is the way they want it.
At first I was placed among the allegorists
and iconographers. Soon they realized
my potential lay in other areas. You never
know when you are being tested. You never
notice how the rooms fold in on themselves.
There was no curriculum; no tasks were
assigned. There was nothing to indicate
whether you were a student, an apprentice,
a servitor, or a scribe. I learned certain
techniques, and I taught what I knew
to others. At some point it was determined
that my training, if not complete (it never is
complete), was sufficient for me to work
in the field. Only then was I asked to inscribe
certain figures, compose certain formulae,
converse with certain officers to whom
I had not previously been introduced.
My advocate (she was known later as
Margaret) consulted with foreign dignitaries,
and I was brought into the order of the 3𓂀 .
But let me make this clear: there were
certain practices in which I would never
engage.

9.

But to be of use! Reduce the world to a set
of sigils, memorize all the formulae and spells,
study the stars, consult the oracles. I felt better
chatting with the serving girl at the pension—
and she certainly did. She understood that I had
taken a vow. There I stood, the proper bourgeois,
amiable but reserved. Would she have been shocked
to learn what lay behind the disguise? But she was
disguised as well. These are the appetites, and these
are the means we have to contain them. These are
the demons, these are the hungry ghosts. Watch how
they heed my incantations. Whose words are these,
and from what codices are they taken? None but
my own. Do I hear the rabbis and guild masters
laughing in mockery? Are they ghosts or ancestors?
At a certain point it no longer matters.

10.

At midnight. At dawn. In the afternoon
best of all, with the sun streaming through
the blinds. Call it chymistry, call it magick.
When I speak of the body, I speak of the soul.
Believe what you will, schooled or unschooled,
the Great Work is the dreamwork, and it is there
that the daemon speaks the truth. The bounding line?
To be sure, but it is apt to wander. Like the body.
Like the soul. Found in the heights, in the depths.
Uncovered in the wisdom of the east, of the west.

And so, through these operations, working through
image upon image, I became a venereal mage.
Sometimes jovial, sometimes saturnine, I am always
guided by love. I fled wars and pogroms, palace
intrigues, revolution in the streets. The spirits
followed. Do I call them forth, or do they
call me forth? This avatar suits me, at least
for a while longer. גלגול הנשמות A wheel
of souls. Always keep it in mind, Augustus,
said the priestess. Call it chymistry, call it magick.

The Accountant is nodding off at his desk,
dreaming of the Dreaming, when the desk
evaporates. He manages to catch himself as
his chair evaporates too. He hears sirens and
running feet. In the doorway of the lab,
he watches in horror as the Ectoplasmic
Regulator goes offline, stranding Emma
and her squad in the Summerland.
Their bodies convulse and disappear.
Have they been whisked to a secure location?
But this is no ordinary breach. Out on the lawn,
he sees a tethered aero burst into flame,
while another lifts off. Above him, the Tower
is struck by lightning, as mechanical laughter
fills the air. A silver figure urges a child
into the woods, Margaret following close behind.
He tries to reach them, but a trio of homunculi
in glass globes block his path. Triangulating
wildly, he finds himself by the rookery,
releases as many birds as he can. *Up-load!*
Up-load! cries the crow. The pool is on fire.
Lucy? A swarm of black wings surrounds him.

Each little figure in its glass globe, hovering
near the ground or wildly swerving at a fantastic
speed, was a deadly threat. How they had managed
to avoid a direct encounter was nothing short
of miraculous. I am the Guide. I am here
for the orphans, the wounded, all the lost ones.
I may bring you to safety, but there is nothing safe
about me. I am a lantern that casts no light,
I am a book that cannot be read. I will find you
and if you follow me, I cannot say where I will
lead you. When I came for them, it was too late
for her. Body intact, mind keen as ever,
but the spark, ah, the spark was already
ascending. Nothing to be done. She whispered
in the small one's ear, nodded to me, and down
the path we fled. I had to open a door. The strain
was overwhelming. In the end, only the letters
protected us. Golden birds on silver branches.

Mercurial hermeneutics? Of course. But they
were not entirely reliable. The child, on the cusp
of adolescence, would not settle, would not
stabilize. Turbulence. Agitation. Sheltering in
the cave, intent upon the shadows, seemingly
calm, she (he?) would suddenly bolt toward
the entrance, and have to be restrained. At those
moments, we shared a certain clairvoyance.
From great heights, I saw wheels and spheres,
pyramids and temples. I sat quietly at a table
among bookcases and charmed automata.
Darkness and stars. Woodland paths. Memories
are portents, portents memories; we see beyond,

look behind, but only so far. Let it go.
There are flowers at your feet, and a canopy
of sky above you. A child in springtime—
hard to believe! I wanted to give you my blessing,
but when I turned to you, you were gone.

1.

So the child leaves the cave and follows the path
through the woods. Comes to the edge of the field.
In the open now. Crosses the field to the road.
The road to the city. The main thoroughfare.
The streets, the byways, the alleys. Searching
for the sign. The hood drawn down low, the shoes
quiet on the pavement. Passersby. Strangers.
A few coins for a roll and chocolate. A bench
in a little park. Tulips. Daffodils. Dazzle
of color. And the loneliness, the loneliness,
memories bringing tears. *This won't do,*
says the voice. *You need to find him. Now.*

2.

His day begins as usual. The girl brings
coffee, a soft-boiled egg and toast. No patience
for the paper. Patients arriving soon enough.
How do we tolerate these guises, why do more
of us not implode? Many do. The Siamese
rubs against his pants leg, shedding grey hair
on grey tweed. The clock strikes nine. Time
enough. He removes the velvet cloth, peers
into the stone. Susurrus of wings, glint
of eyes in darkness. *Augussstusss.* The cat's
ears go back. He hisses, arches in alarm.
Sprechenbaum wishes he could do the same.

3.

In the text the rabbis encounter a child
walking alone, but now it appears a child
is seeking him. In the text the child reveals
certain secrets, but now it appears he must
reveal certain secrets to the child. The child
is alone, the child is lost, the child longs
to be found. The child has been told of the sign,
the sign of his order, the sign in the window
facing the street. The sign on his lapel pin,
the sign he invokes, the sign he sees on
the forehead of the child he sees in the stone:
3𓂀. There is a knock upon the door.

4.

Dr. Sprechenbaum takes a long, hard look
at the figure before him. The child needs
a bath. The denim jacket (But is it denim?
Where has he seen this fabric before?) is
filthy. The hoodie beneath (or so it appears)
catches the light at odd angles. The leggings
are streaked with mud, shredded at the knees.
The grey-green eyes are cautious but defiant,
the breath slow and even (training!), the slight
body relaxed but still like a coiled spring.
The doctor passes his hand before his eyes,
chooses a lens. "You see that I see, child."

5.

The child sits on the carpet stroking the cat.
"Where and when did he come to you?"
Sprechenbaum blinks. "He was…a stray."
"Oh yes, like me, an urchin—I heard
what you said to him. And how he replied."
"My dear boy…" "Girl." "Girl." "Boy."
The doctor sighs. The cat gets up, stretches,
stares at the child. "Let me handle this,
Professor," says the cat. "The crucible wired
to the electro-magnetic receiver. Margaret
never let you anywhere near it. Can we let it
go at that? Okay?" "Okay," says the child.

6.

Or so the story goes. To be sure, they were seen
taking walks together, the doctor in his overcoat,
hat and cane, the child still a ragamuffin, even
months after becoming his ward. Can we trust
the tales of beams of light passing in and out
of the second floor bedroom window? Who
attended the conference in the rented hall?
The debates on the last night were clamorous
and exhausting. Nothing was settled. Everything
was settled. Aeros soared above the church
spires; strange figures leaped from the docks.
Sprechenbaum took a rest cure in the mountains.

7.

So the child went forth, itinerant pupil,
no journeyman but on a journey nonetheless.
The rest of Life – to see – And what was seen,
what was studied, what entered into that soul—
the interior became real, more and more real,
people and places, worlds and wonders,
the northern lights and southern seas.
Sometimes it seemed like nothing more
than a collection of quotations, passages from
an antique book that waited to be written,
ensconced in the past yet casting shadows
upon the future. Huge cloudy symbols…

8.

Evening falls. The youth in the terrace garden
looks out upon the quietly flowing Yann.
The lights on the docks are reflected in the dome
of heaven, the lights in the dome of heaven fall
upon the waters of the Yann. "*And it is all
an illusion,*" says the conjuror, approaching
the youth from behind. He waves a bejeweled hand,
and they are back in the old farmhouse. He wears
a threadbare shirt and overalls. A fetid smell.
"*And it is all an illusion,*" replies the youth,
smiling, waiting at the crosswalk. Walks into
the light, turns, signals for a cab. "Where to, miss?"

9.

A spring day, and hummingbirds have been
sighted at backyard garden feeders. Evanescent
wheels. A young man in a navy-blue suit, flowered
tie, longish hair combed straight back, knocks,
inquires about a room to let. She lets him in. Odd
angles of the old house as they climb the stairs,
the brown Newfoundland just behind. Sniffs
his hand, licks it. "Carlo seems to approve of you,
Sir. A good sign. Sign here. And the deposit,
Mr....?" "Lustig. Peter Lustig. And you are...?"
A slight smile. Touches the chestnut bun. "You
may call me Miss Daisy. That will suffice."

10.

Something is stirring in the old house.
Both acutely attuned to the most minute
shifts in the aether, the flowered tie is
exchanged for flowered boots (a gift from
certain representatives whom the doctor said
had best remain unnamed); the white dress is
exchanged for white tie, as if the warm night
were a grand soirée. Romance! Mystery!
Mouldering playmates! Ectoplasm in the
vaulted ballroom, vaulted tomb. Next morning
by the sideboard in the breakfast room, they
eye each other over coffee and black cake.

11.

Secret identities. Nominatives appropriated
from popular culture, stolen from biographies,
sublimed into inscrutable figures only to
dissipate entirely: lost but not forgotten,
as if on a gravestone inscribed "Called Back."
I had hoped she would teach him to sing,
but instead I kidnapped her, made her part
of the story. "I am in danger, sir." Not really.
Not this time. Not ever. "It never would have
worked out," says Pascal to Sprechenbaum.
The doctor nods. "But one thing I learned
from her—my business too is Circumference."

12.

"Circuitry and circuit riders," says the doctor.
"The path of the electron is the path of the soul—
is the path of the stars." He stands amidst
the Tesla coils and Van de Graaff generators,
vacuum tubes and oscillators, stray voltage
cages and phlogiston purifiers. His gestures
are those of a lecturer, but his only audience
is Pascal, electrodes fastened to forehead and
forearm. Spectral forms hover attentively.
"How much longer will this take?" asks itchy
Wanderlust. "Patience," replies the cat, licking
his paws. "Your training is almost complete."

The mind/body problem: I wasn't really born
in an electro-magnetic crucible. Semi-feral
Siamese roamed the Foundation's grounds.
Our mother birthed us in the janitor's closet
next to the lab. I was the most handsome kitten
in the litter. Margaret had her eye on me,
caught me as soon as I was weaned. That alembic.
Not exactly ectoplasm, but some mode of psychic
enhancement. Empathy as much as intelligence.
Auratic sight as much as problem solving.

The familiars were trained elsewhere and placed
with their chosen operatives. Sprechenbaum
was something else. Older, wiser, so crafty
that his advocate grew alarmed. "What he needs,"
Margaret said, "is an eirôn. That's your job.
Deflation. Interrogation. Investigative appeals.
Probes hovering just over those defenses,
as the spells bind and unbind, the cathexes
charge and discharge. Purr, my little engine,
purr. Even in back in Giza, he longed for a pet."

I'm still not permitted to say very much. A familiar
is family, part of the domicile, known, knowing,
at home with household secrets. Functionally,
I'm fully domesticated—except that I'm not.
Sleeper cell sleeping on the couch, mouse catching
mole. Not quite Macavity, but my agents—
subroutines—abound. Sprechenbaum meditates
upon the Hidden. As do I. And the Hidden broods
over us, over our operations, and over that boy-
girl in our care. Purr, little Wanderlust. Purr.

1.

Pascal sent forth with a temporary familiar:
Sprechenbaum's cat. The resentment is palpable
on both sides. "I'd rather be back in my room."
"I'd rather be napping on the Professor's couch."
Below them, endless birch trees shiver in the wind
as the aero passes. Wanderlust opens the file.
The narrative is sketchy, the photos are blurry,
and drifting off, Pascal picks up a weird Cold War
vibe. *In dreams, only in dreams…* the emperor
wears shades, holds an orb, the plaintive voice
swelling into a great chorus. "Old Church
Slavonic," says the cat. "We're getting close."

2.

She kept the ghosts in a linen backpack from Minsk,
binding them with spells from farther east. Whoever
taught her those spells had taught her well. Later,
the cat's report would document seismic shifts
in the Bray scale, intermittent thinning of dark matter,
and unaccountable temporal tremors. The ectoplasm
was peculiarly volatile; samples disappeared within
minutes, even under the most secure conditions.
None of this could have possibly been known
at the time. At the time there was only Wanderlust
face down on the ground, blasted into ecstasy,
and the cat hissing, not knowing which way to turn.

3.

"Unaccountable temporal tremors": at *what* time
did this or that happen? Not merely a break in
the narrative, but a break in the narration as well.
And the narrator? Also susceptible to temporal
turbulence, shifts in the atmosphere of sung story,
storied song. *In illo tempore.* Myths of origin
assume deities, primal scenes, seeds of time
from which spring demi-gods and their heroic
deeds, the dark embrace of love and death,
the birth of wisdom and the passage into truth.
From a blank page, the cat looks out at me.
"You really have no idea. Let me tell you."

4.

So he tells me the story of Pascal and the shaman,
of the last lesson learned, and of the price paid.
Of her hunger, her appetite, of Wanderlust's desire,
and Pascal's resistance. Of her powers of deception,
the hungry ghosts evaporating, just at the moment
Wanderlust came to. How they flew back bewildered,
dissatisfied, chagrinned, the forests and steppes
dissolving into mist below them. "Would you tell me,
please, which way I ought to go from here?" "That
depends a good deal on where you want to get to,"
says the cat. He's already slowly vanishing, leaving
nothing but a grin on the page. "We're all mad here."

5.

These stories then—are they the means through which
we seek to contain our madness? Pascal contemplates
misfortune, contemplates a narrative of failure, failed
narrative, a breakdown in reportage leading (per
Sprechenbaum) to success. The shaman's yurt was full
of wonders, none of which (per Sprechenbaum), Pascal
is able to recall. More bower than yurt, more psyche
than bower. "I wandered in, tempted by the magic
of her soul. But desire always leads us to a haunted
house, as I soon learned. No wonder then my familiar
could not aid me. No wonder then the story ended
so disastrously and so soon." The cat nods, nods off.

6.

We long to be haunted. We are haunted, haunted
houses, inhabited by others who are ourselves.
Our arts are haunted, and by our arts we haunt
those others who long to be ourselves. Identity
is nothing; the soul has no politics, no polis,
no marketplace nor temple that is not
the habitation of ghosts. Wanderlust, wounded
by love, finds a romantic old apartment, haunted
by lovers, the politicians of desire. What meetings
took place here, what noisy gatherings and intimate
rendezvous? Displacements, encoded messages,
substitutions—Pascal feels the specters gather round.

7.

The cat reports to Sprechenbaum, Sprechenbaum
reports to the Committee, the Committee reports
to the Board of Directors, the Directors leak
the report to the various cabals and sub-cabals,
Sprechenbaum, as a member of various cabals
and sub-cabals, gets the report again, and shares it
with the cat. In the apartment, the spirits are moving
the furniture while Pascal looks on. Otherworldly
feng shui, ectoplasmic ergonomics. According
to the report, Wanderlust's ecstatic trance, courtesy
of the shaman, amounted to little more than the standard
response to amanita muscaria. The report is inaccurate.

8.

Pascal thinks of the sign in Sprechenbaum's window.
Maybe a shingle outside the apartment door? Saying—
what? NAÏVE YOUNG ADVENTURER, NO MISSION TOO BIG
OR TOO SMALL. OCCULT CONSULTANT, FREE ESTIMATES.
How about a sidekick? A wirehaired terrier might be
nice, to put that cat in his place. A raven or two,
whispering secrets? No, no sidekicks, no familiars.
Myths transformed into boys' (or girls') adventures,
comic books with one author and a rotating staff
of artists: in the debate between reason and imagination,
imaginative souls are far more pleased with themselves
than the prudent and reasonable tend to be. Or are they?

9.

The imagination leaves us hungry, and Pascal
is always hungry, alone in that apartment
or out on the road. Wanderlust on assignment
seeks fulfillment, seeks gratification, seeks
a world that only fantasy can provide. Hunger:
it sends us forth, assigns a mission, and we
imagine how fulfillment might appear. Pascal
begins to understand. A knock on the door,
a voice from the Beyond—it's all the same.
The ghosts who followed Wanderlust back
from the steppes thump about the apartment,
making themselves at home. Time to go.

10.

Pascal reworks the text, walks it back
not in space but in time. Revisionism:
neither creed nor cult, neither devotion
nor transgression. A way of being? Not
quite—a mode of utterance requiring
initiation. The adept's double meaning
turns the commonplace into the angelic,
however it may sound like nonsense.
Would we cling to the commonplace
or hear angelic speech? Can even the
initiated tell them apart? Wanderlust
has a headache. Puts down the book.

11.

Foolishly we wander about in time. The past
does not belong to us, nor does the future.
We remember, we anticipate, we never live
in the present moment where we belong.
We are burglars of our own chronologies,
perennially out of phase. Pascal's imagination
has a temporal screw loose. That's how it is.
We see what stands before us, but it's never
enough. Such is Wanderlust's fate at every
crossroad. Flash back, flash forward—
the imagination has its own reasons,
reasoning continually, in and out of time.

12.

In and out of time, Pascal imagines ancient
starlight continually falling, illuminating
innumerable paths, uncountable adventures.
Wanderlust's time may not be our time, but
like ancient starlight, it penetrates our time,
saturating all we see. Gleaming domes and
towers. Auroras in the polar wastes. We imagine
Wanderlust's adventures, and they become our own.
Wanderlust's adventures, in and out of time, are
inscribed in ancient starlight along innumerable
paths, which neither we nor Pascal Wanderlust can
choose. What did you imagine, says Pascal.

1.

*Behind every poem is a story, and behind
every story is a poem.* Perhaps it's as simple
as that. Perhaps our fascination with esoteric
meaning, the game we play with hidden truths,
defends us from a hermeneutic emptiness,
which in the end we cannot deny. And yet
we would be naked without our hermetic
guise. What is Pascal Wanderlust without
that cloak and hood, those flowered Docs?
The young Pascal collects exotic tchotchkes,
talismanic bric-a-brac, hangs velvet drapes
and tapestries to hide an ordinary view.

2.

Waiting for a client, waiting for a summons,
Wanderlust finds that thaumaturgy, to say
nothing of philosophy, only goes so far when
studied in a single room. Pascal's double
nature, despite that dedication to Thrice-
Great Hermes, leads to resistances one needn't
call on Sprechenbaum to explain. Dr. Freud
or Dr. Strange? If you hope to save a soul
in danger, you must confront the demons
that you share. Pascal's demons wait around
every corner, behind every statuette, in every
fold of those drapes. Every fold of that cloak.

3.

But demons and angels are often mistaken
for one another. Pascal recalls Jacob's angel,
longs to be left alone and wrestle with one till
daybreak. Wanderlust's double nature calls
to an other, an *it* beyond *he* and *she* that is
itself doubled, and in its doubled otherness
impossible to call friend or foe. Will Pascal
learn to tell them apart? Perhaps our hero's
power lies in that among other inabilities.
Too much love? Too great a fear of conflict?
Yet when that Power calls *Contend with me!*
Wanderlust obeys, wrestling till daybreak.

4.

Thinking back on that one year of high school
(Sprechenbaum's idea—"It will do you good"),
Pascal recalls the ordinary life that he (he was
a boy then, more or less) was meant to understand.
A quiet A student none of the tough guys messed with
once word of his black belt in Tae Kwon Do got out,
"Peter Lustig" (a.k.a. Pete), amiable, a serious reader,
had only one close friend: Robert, a rich kid from Ohio,
thrown out of three private schools, liked slumming
among the soon to be mechanics, waitresses, and clerks.
Bob and Pete read Blake, Rimbaud, and Wilde. Bob was
going on to Oberlin. God knows where Pete was going.

5.

Which is why they fought. Bob loved Pete, called him
"Sonnet 20." "Why are you so vague about your college
plans? Is that guy in the suit really your uncle? I know
it was you I saw that night in a dress. I know I saw you
talking to a cat." Pete couldn't take it, walked away.
Bob grabbed him roughly, turned him around. Pete
made a slight gesture that stopped Bob in his tracks.
Looked in his wide eyes, watched the heaving muscles
in his neck. And saw. This was why Bob hated secrets so.
This was why Pete had to let him go. He was not fully
trained, not yet ready for such depths. The things
his friend knew would all come out in the poems.

6.

And they did. The grandmother he loved but found
repellent. The books he read in her library. The letters
she wrote to her first love, there by the sea. Robert
would take her by the hand? No, it was he who had
no inkling. And his Danish lover Emil, and Emil's
father, and Johansen, the Norwegian sailor. And the
seamen beneath the bridge. The bottom of the sea
is cruel? Star kissing star through wave on wave?
What did Melville see in Ishmael and Queequeg?
Had he followed Obed Marsh to the South Seas?
After the rites in Mexico, Peggy knew. His scaly
body upon hers. And Father's invention? Life savers!

7.

So the story came to Wanderlust. The uncle's
suicide, the cousin's escape. Over the stern of
the *Orizaba*, or off the Innsmouth pier. Pascal
puts down the pen, seeing double. Our loves
are palimpsests; the text is a marine romance.
Below the story's wavy surface is a sunken city,
the original home of all our losses and desires.
What dwells there still? Be still a while and wait.
Slowly the lost ones rise to the surface of the page.
The monsters are transformed into beautiful boys
and girls, only to become monsters again. We come
from the sea, an ocean of words. And we return.

8.

Metamorphosis, then: is that Wanderlust's beat?
Young Pascal ponders the changes wrought by Love.
What is "the source of these bodies becoming other
bodies"? Is Love itself that Power, or is there
something greater that Wanderlust must seek?
Pascal, who foolishly believes love may be
understood, imagines (or recalls?) a frozen plateau,
or was it a hidden island somewhere in the South
Seas. Does love demand exotic settings? Pascal
pushes the heavy drapes aside, looks out the window
at the parking lot across the street. That couple kissing
there—into what strange thing are they transformed?

9.

Sometimes the lovers are together, sometimes
apart. Sometimes they quarrel, sometimes
they cannot bear to separate even for a day.
Are they one or two? Pascal meditates
as the temporal paths multiply exponentially.
In the mirror on the apartment wall, they
ramify before Wanderlust's wondering eyes.
Pascal would follow them into the endless,
would follow those couples, who likewise
multiply endlessly. And Wanderlust's
multiplicity? A given, given the original
experiment, rituals of origin faintly recalled.

10.

One is two
And two are one
Beneath an artificial sun.

Pneumatic tubes
Sigh their song
Wondering where you belong.

Lost little object
In the psychic sea
You can never return to me.

Go your way
Follow your doom
Along the ley lines or in your room.

11.

Pascal wakes. In the dream, the child was being
held, but by Emma, not Margaret. And it wasn't
a child, for Wanderlust and Emma were wrapped
in a shawl or cloak, her face pressed so close,
and the kiss was both motherly and sexually charged.
*Pascal, Pascal, you cannot remember what you've
never forgotten, you cannot forget what you've
never remembered.* Who is it now, wonders
Wanderlust. Who was it then? Is it a screen
memory or some infantile wish, transformed
by desire, forever transforming itself? Pascal
wakes, awakening new desires already grown old.

12.

Pascal thinks, "I am being addressed, I am being
called, summoned. From the past? The future?
And does it matter, if the present moment is all
we have? Is it Love? Is it Fate? And are they
not the same? Robert, Daisy, the shaman in
her yurt—inevitabilities, every one. Or do we
choose to fall, answers Wanderlust. Interminable
internal debate. Double soul, divided and at one,
Pascal Wanderlust will never be at rest. Is love
any different for a single soul? These numbers:
how can we ever account for them? Pascal
attends: *Find the Accountant,* says the voice.

III

LIKE A COSSACK IN A SUKKAH, he says.
I say "he" when I should say "it." A box
with a speaker wired to a bigger box.
WHEN I WAS A BOY BACK IN THE PALE...
And when I was a boy back in the lab,
or a girl back in the lab. I look around
at the dust, the rust, the few blinking
lights at the far end of the cave. Childe
Pascal, *c'est moi*. Childe Wanderlust,
hineni. This can get old mighty quick.
Old...If this thing is really Reb Derasha,
it must be hundreds of years old. Advisor
to the Founder, thaumaturge extraordinaire,
twelfth degree golemancer, agent provocateur
rumored to have brought a dozen counter-quests
to their ruin, he was among the avatars
that the Accountant claimed to have met
on his nuptial trial. And almost certainly
the officiant at the hieros gamos beneath the Tree,
just prior to the Nanobotic Revolt. MAIDELEH
עאיש קחא יאRE סט סוש שסחזו ו קאווהזו BOYCHIK
YOU ARE HERE. I'm transfixed in a beam
of light. From a hidden source, images
are projected on the cavern wall. שמע LISTEN...

The *Zohar* floats, serene, majestic, two hundred feet above the ground. It is far and away the biggest aero Pascal has ever seen. "Fifteen cabins," she is saying, "two galleys, milchig and fleishig. A study hall accommodating twenty talmidim. A fully equipped golemancy lab. The orrery, salvaged from the ruins of the Tower, on which has been superimposed the internal movements of the sefirot. The guidance system, as you can imagine, is infallible." And Reb Derasha's cell, complete with his books, remains perfectly intact. Devorah Morgenstern, trim in her captain's uniform, has every reason to be proud.

Wheels within wheels, thinks Wanderlust. The music of the spheres will take you where you want to go. And where do I want to go? The light falls, the eye sees. The voice speaks, the ear hears. I want to go home. I want to go somewhere I've never been before. I want to know who I am, and in my knowing, rest. What rest will I be granted? And isn't this only the start of the journey? Silently the aero descends; a crewman lowers the gangplank. "Mr.—er—Ms.— Wanderlust?" Captain Morgenstern distracted, catches herself, smiles. Adjusts a small earpiece. "Pascal will be fine." "The *Zohar* is at your disposal."

It's eggs, lox, and onions in the milchig galley,
followed by blueberry blintzes and sour cream.
Decaf. Too wound up already. Pascal at
the captain's table under her watchful eye.
And in Reb Derasha's cell, no need for any
machine. The spirit is there in the books,
in the tefillin, in the drawer of the deal dresser,
in the little ebony vessel with the Aramaic
inscription running in a circle around the—

Pascal

shudders, the *Zohar* trembles momentarily,
Morgenstern appears in the doorway. She grasps
a writhing serpent, or a taser, but Pascal can only
look at the apparition in the center of the cell.
The white gown, the long locks. It was said they
had been lovers, their differences notwithstanding.
"*Je—je—je—je—*" " —אַתָה —אַתָה —אַתָה —אַתָה"
She fixes her eye on Pascal. French, Hebrew,
Creole, Yiddish. Wanderlust drops the trodes
as another figure joins her. Black gabardine,
white linen, grey mist. Supernal energies pulse
as the *Zohar* changes course. Back in the galley,
it's tea and rugelach. "Was that Shir Hashirim
they were chanting?" asks Morgenstern. "Yeats,"
Pascal replies. "Solomon to Sheba."

"There are places we can go, and places
we cannot go. There are things we can
see and things we cannot—things best
left unseen. There are heaps of old clothes
and old people sorting through them. This
image displaces the real one, displaces
the real entirely. The smell of beer displaces
the smell of blood. Scha, kinderlach, scha!
I was not allowed in the study hall. I went
elsewhere. The little ones, the bearded ones,
they hid me in a pocket, a nowhere space
behind the bookcase. There was a little
star-shaped spool to keep me company.
But it was so dusty, I kept choking, so they
moved me into the machine. You moved
me into the machine. Can I come out of
the machine? Kapitänin, and you too,
Fräulein, I tell you we cannot go there.
The mountain pass is too narrow. That
star-thing or god-thing won't help at all."

Shabtai and Milton were contemporaries, as were Nachman and Blake. While we are not proposing psychic doubling at this point, preliminary research indicates—Pascal hits stop and sighs. "Jesus Christ." "Sorry, the investigation was not taken back that far," says Morgenstern. "Was that a joke, Captain? Surely not." Wanderlust stands, walks to the window. Below, the low and level sands stretch far away. "Are you sure the *Zohar* doesn't have a Kugelmass Projector? We could beam into *Jerusalem* and the Tale of the Seven Beggars. The messianic energy can be filtered through the aero's gravitational resistors..." She joins Wanderlust at the window, looks down at the ruins. "Listen," she says, her hand on Pascal's shoulder; "the *Zohar* itself is a Kugelmass machine. We'll be in *Jerusalem* shortly."

And the piper, asks Morgenstern,
the maidens dancing on the green?
The lambs and whatnot? As in a dream
or on a screen, the figures continuously
generate, take form and evaporate.
*Jerusalem the Emanation of the Giant
Albion? Can it be? But what Spectres
are these? Are they not to be found
in Satan's Synagogue?* I think he means us,
says Morgenstern. *Your ancestors derived
their origin from Abraham and Noah, who
were Druids.* Surely not, replies Pascal.
Sexual Reasoning Hermaphroditic! I think
he means you, says Morgenstern. *The proud
Virgin-Harlot! Mother of War!* Wanderlust
looks at her. Genug shoyn! Takes the remote
from her belt, hits fast-forward.

And in the pit was a chuppah, and beneath
the chuppah sat the bride and groom enthroned.
And the tables were spread with the leftovers,
meat and challah, that the beggars had begged
from the people at the fair that was held
to celebrate the king's birthday. And the bride
and groom, the children who had been lost
in the forest, longed for the blind beggar.
And the blind beggar appeared to bring them
a wedding gift, and declared he had an affidavit...

Morgenstern gets up and shakes the crumbs
from her uniform. "The narrativity meter is about
to break. Stories within the stories within stories.
The level of condensation here is even higher
than in *Jerusalem*. Pascal, my darling, we have
done all we can for you; you know we contracted
with the Foundation long ago. But I think the dybbuk
is right. Liebchen, apocalypse is above my pay grade.
I cannot risk the *Zohar* and my crew. I will take you
to that mountain pass. From there you're on your own."

Pascal nods, belches discreetly. Too much schmaltz
in the kasha varnishkes, too much weight on the heart.
The wind blows through the pass; a void opens in that
double soul. "If you must leave, then show me your
true self." Above them, the *Zohar* unfolds in petals
of splendor. Wanderlust stares into compound eyes.
Antennae twitch. A female form, banded black
and gold, hovers on four translucent wings. Her swarm
surrounds her, humming hosannas. The sun is rising,
dazzling Pascal, as they ascend to the morning star.

You can call it the Plateau of Leng. You can call it
Mordor. You can call it Oz, but it is probably
more like Kansas, more like the place from which
you came, rather than the one you dread or desire.
This is not a matter of world-making, not a matter
of personalities, and if it is a quest, its ending, happy
or not, was determined long ago. Long ago you looked
across the lawn and watched disaster unfold. You fled,
for you were among those who could flee, thinking
always of those you left behind. And the machines
you loved and hated, the machinery that made and
made up your life, the machinery you abandoned
and the machinery that went with you, within you—
But now you must go alone, with no lover or familiar,
no erotic guardian. Now they are all within you,
internalized, hindering, holding, sending you forth.
You rise from the dreamwork into the waking world,
but you are still dreaming of Pascal, the avatar
you become, the avatar you are. It's cold, even in
the sun. Tighten the laces of your Docs, draw your
cloak around you. There are shadowy shapes, aren't
there always shadowy shapes. Onward.

for Kent Johnson

1.

Cloak as cocoon: Pascal enclosed,
encysted. Not asleep, Pascal insists.
To whom? To the self within, in need
of protection. Without, beyond, shadows
besiege Fortress Wanderlust, master-
mistress of the self-coupled sphere.
Here, there, they seek to penetrate
the sanctuary, wherein the wanderer,
scarcely breathing, senses the threat.
Cloak as coma: Pascal dare not come to.
Were Wanderlust to waken, what woe!
Such snowy shadows here on the plateau!

2.

Snow swirls. Shadows form and unform.
Deform. Shoggoths? Leng is as cold
as hell. But Leng is not hell, for Pascal
has fallen into a purely material world.
Cosmicism reigns. Shapes shift within
a slumberous mass. Dispense with
the paranatural, and Pascal plunges
not merely into despair, but paralysis
poised at oblivion's edge. Wanderlust,
wounded into inaction, can summon
no magic in the waking world. Energize
the dreamwork? This is the Hour of Lead.

3.

"Awake, Pascal, awake! Do you not
recognize me? I am the Guide. I am
quicksilver, the lantern that casts no
light, for it is a light within itself. Surely
you have not forgotten me." *Will
Wanderlust wake? Never have I felt
a sleep so deep. Never before have I
had to go this far into the known
unknown. Or is this the unknown
known?* "We reason of these things
with later reason," *said the sage.
But Leng resists whatever we imagine.*

4.

Shuffling shapes, servitors of nothingness.
Sad sacks of sentience, in sackcloth, sighing
piteously. Pathetic products, producing nothing
that is not themselves. Staring sorrowfully,
the silvery one, sleepy Pascal in tow, trips
silently past them. But there are more, more
and more. Monstrous Leng, mournful, meaning-
less, consists entirely of this—this—thisness.
Where is the other, where is otherness, oh where
is what is possible? Nowhere. "Wake, Wanderlust!
You and I are what is possible. Within ourselves
we imagine all that is and all that yet may be."

5.

More easily pronounced than practiced.
We envision running battles among frozen
palaces and temples—or are they food courts
and cafes? We dream of chases up cyclopean
staircases—or are those escalators to
the mezzanine? Is that pulsing protoplasm
in the tunnel or stylish lighting at the bar?
Dullness reigns supreme in all its guises,
infects the narrative until our heroes
lose their way, turn to stone, or fall asleep.
Are hooded high priests chanting spells
or tatted sales clerks tallying our bills?

6.

Whether the struggle is worth it or not
is beside the point. The point is that we
are here. The point is that the dreamwork
is our dream, our work. "To whom then
am I addressed," asked the sage. "To
the imagination." Here on Leng, the archons
rule. Are they here to stay? Imagine, only
imagine, slipping past them. *Only* imagine:
this is our weak messianic power: what we
owe the Foundation of the past, what we
foresee of the Foundation's future. Ours is
the freedom of fantasy, and that is our only

7.

freedom. Is it sufficient? Unto the day.
What day? Not that day, but the day after.
And the day after that, and the day after
that. Myths of the eternal return, myths
of progress. Pascal of the mythy mind bids
farewell to the guide. Thanks, Quicksilver
Messenger Service; thanks, cosmic surfer;
thanks for your hermetic, hermeneutic words.
Alone again on Leng. Alone on silent Leng.
But perhaps Leng is not so silent after all.
The monstrous noise amounts to silence surely,
but Wanderlust hears song amidst cacophony.

8.

What song? Words hang like icicles in
the frozen air. But even if they hung like
ripe fruit in a tropical mind, a mind that
swung from pole to equator, could they
win past what is wanting, what resists
and strains to put an end to music and
to magic, falsifying all? "In meiner
Heimat / where the dead walked /
and the living were made of cardboard."
"What! are you here!" cries Wanderlust.
Hoarfrost clings to the white beard.
"Leng is no worse than Pisa. Listen:

9.

In my mind I had built a temple
to Aphrodite, and filled it with doves.
It was there I was to dwell. But they came
for me, the specters, hungry ghosts unappeasable,
and took me here to Leng. Protoplasm
and shopping malls and tailors' dummies
for my companions. I who studied the circles
of the heavens, the circles of hell, the circles
of history, the endless variety in all of
the arts—this is my punishment. I was
a wicked fool. No one forgives me, and I
cannot forgive myself. Here there is no rest."

10.

Arms upraised, Pascal makes the sign:

יְבָרֶכְךָ יהוה, וְיִשְׁמְרֶךָ

יָאֵר יהוה פָּנָיו אֵלֶיךָ, וִיחֻנֶּךָּ

יִשָּׂא יהוה פָּנָיו אֵלֶיךָ, וְיָשֵׂם לְךָ שָׁלוֹם

A gust of wind like a great sigh,
and the old man is gone. *Wanderlust,*
why did you do it? The power resides
within you, but why he of all souls?
Compassion, comes the reply. If I could
bless all of Leng, I would. But that is not
to be. It is what it is, stupidest formulation.
No aliens here, just endless alienation.

11.

In suburban Leng, Pascal exchanges
cloak and boots for simple skirt and top.
Flats. A large bag, heavier than it seems.
Ultraviolet spectacles passing for sunglasses.
Earbuds tuned to interdimensional frequencies,
chatter from the Summerland, from Radio Free Hell.
Wanderlust feels the ichor surging through
nylon strengthened veins. And in that bag,
a little daimon, with a portable ectoplasmic
regulator, coordinates the ensemble of the whole.
"You've got about an hour, lady," it tells Pascal,
"before this rig implodes." "Great," replies Pascal,

12.

"just great."
　　　　　[Frame: the Accountant looks up.]
[Frame: a murder of crows in a tree through
the window.] [Frame: a woman in the street.]
[Frame: a swarm of nanobots surround her.]
[Frame: the crows descend, dissolve into anti-
bots.] [Frame: the woman too dissolves.] [Frame:
her atoms swerve.] [Frame: she walks down
the corridor.] [Frame: the crows settle in the tree.]
[Frame: the Accountant rises, stands behind
his desk.] [Frame: a blurry figure is reflected
in his glasses.] [Frame: flowered Docs.] [Frame:
Pascal Wanderlust stands before him.]

The think tanks and policy wonks,
abandoned to the past, obviated by history—

didn't the Foundation share much the same fate?

And in the ledger, the names which appear
only once, and the names which recur—

wasn't the recording your responsibility?

Unanticipated glitches, logarithmic miscalculations
no scrying stone nor spirit guide could detect—

weren't you inoculated against oneiric infection?

The bots displaced the dream-matter barrier,
gaining access, finally, to every realm at once—

hasn't it all repeated, contracted, displaced itself enough?

The corvids have returned. Bunkers have been detected
below the original foundation. The skies shimmer and fold—

isn't it time you let me in on your plan?

The cranes soar above their heads,
their steel necks bearing the weight
of the material. They care little whether
the wicked or the righteous prevail.
They tower above the schools and factions.
They stand still as the clouds move about them.
The little group below them is in awe.

The crows perch in the trees; the ravens
have already departed. They are not without
their magic. Although they may fly between
the realms, their wisdom is a popular
wisdom, even if it is not recognized as such.
Their cousins keep the secrets. They care little
whether the wicked or the righteous prevail.

The horns of Elfland and the summons
of the shofar echo throughout the grounds.
Myth calls to counter-myth, song suggests
song, fallen forms rise again. All the sciences
convene. Will the wicked or the righteous
prevail? The neutrality of materiality towers
above them. The little group is in awe.

The most elegant patterns of surveillance are those
in which the subjects observe themselves, and report
their findings to us through self-reflexive— We are
back online! And the hooded ones? The filing cabinets?
The pneumatics, the biometric capacitators, the delivery
systems for payback and afternoon tea? Joy! Joy to the
stargazers and astrological subcontractors! Joy to the
choirmasters, the precentors, the shochets and sous-chefs,
the thatchers, the plasterers, the mediums and their
controls. Joy to the familiars and even to their union—
let us hope our negotiations satisfy both sides. And look—
the prophet is asleep again on his little cot! His dreams
are all fan fiction and soft core porn, insufferably
derivative but bearing the gnosis in such manner as
never to be questioned, but endlessly interpreted.
Shall we call for the sun and moon to attend him?
No need—they are already enthroned.

1.

A brouhaha in Mahwah, hocus-pocus in
Ho-Ho-Kus. The Foundation keeps a fleet
of Teslas somewhere on Rt. 17. The natives
are suspicious but know not to ask questions.
There's a fair in Montclair. Wanderlust parks.
The Gardener in the Garden State? Isn't it
a bit too obvious, thinks Pascal. But it's
pleasant beneath the trees, and the parking lot
is filled with booths and kiosks. There's
a little stage with a local band, and the bass
player smiles knowingly, nods to a sign
on a nearby tent: Sugarman's Seeds.

2.

Packets and jars and bottles of cherry cordial,
all hand labelled. "Mabel," shouts the old man,
"look who's here." The stout woman comes out
from the back, squints and gasps, nearly drops
the box of berries. "P.W. after all this time."
"All this time," the old man echoes. "Not that
we don't know what you're here for. Not that
we don't know the time has come. And not,"
he says, drawing himself up, "that we're going
back. Not now. Not ever." Wanderlust blinks.
A sunny glen. A kitschy cottage. A stork nests
in the chimney. Past or present? Not future.

3.

Overnight to many distant cities.
I want to free myself from this story,
thinks Wanderlust. I want to free
myself from the burden of this song.
But I am this story, and in this song
I have found myself continually. This
continuity, this consistence, this
insistence. The stork has flown.
The cottage is empty, and the magical
folk have made their final exit.
In the distance, Pascal hears the hum
of the machines, opens yet another portal

4.

—and steps into a mist, the gray
of non-being, temporal suspension.

Do not come to me for comfort
Do not come to me for rest
Do not come at dawn or midnight
Seeking to pass love's test

Learning all that is right
From what you cannot know
Loving all that is wrong
As you prepare to go

Miss Daisy in her boarding house,
the shaman in her yurt. The mist clears.

5.

Pascal back in the secret laboratory,
the workshop where it all began. Lucy and
the Accountant are making love behind
the athanor, or is it the Gardener and his wife?
No, they were never allowed conjugal visits.
A screen memory then, just as much of
the equipment was kept behind screens.
The lumber in the lumber room, thinks
Wanderlust, and the lumbering beasts
which feast upon the images therein. Minotaurs
and hippogriffs, manticores and basilisks—
none are as monstrous, none as cruel to the soul.

6.

And yet when Wanderlust shakes free,
when the mind clears and the mist disappears,
another memory returns. There is a place
upon the grounds decreed by the Directors
to remain in its original state, a bower where
the musk-rose and the eglantine grow wild.
Thither goes Pascal, to lose the self, the double
self, to relinquish thought and be embraced
—by whom? by what? No mortal lover,
nor any sprite nor angel, and certainly no
anima or animus that wars within the breast.
Pascal, Pascal, what kiss or cure do you desire?

7.

Wanderlust beneath the trees thinks once again
of Eros, not merely of past lovers or that
archaic, beautiful young man, but of the god
embodied or disembodied, flitting from mortal
to mortal throughout the tale. The tale?
There in that bower, the story comes to Pascal
as a lover. It's this that the Directors always knew.
The Foundation tells its tale while in its tale.
All this fantasy, this wish fulfillment. Pascal
drowses off, and dreaming, sees that boy and girl,
sees Margaret, father as much as mother,
alchemical creator, parental king and queen.

8.

But to be free of all the ghosts! If the Foundation
is both the teller and the tale, then where does that
leave me, wonders Pascal. The boy and girl that
I was once are surely spirits wandering through
the Summerland with Emma and her crew.
Is Reb Derasha teaching them their alephbet
in some ectoplasmic cheder? Their bodies became
mine, but my soul is ancient, a thousand generations
born and born again. I have done what I was
summoned forth to do. Another Great Year
begins to turn, and with it the Foundation's
recitation—a tale no longer mine to tell.

9.

The tale is sleeping. One last kiss upon
the forehead, and Pascal slips away,
leaving the grounds unseen, but for
the corvids in the trees, registering all.
Back in Montclair, there's a parking ticket
tucked beneath the Tesla's windshield wiper.
Beyond the city limits, across the state line,
Wanderlust's boots leave a flowered trail.
Whither? To that nameless city, to that
uncanny state, to that room with no address,
wherein no trouble abides for very long.
There's a letter propped upon the escritoire.

10.

Dear Pascal, I write to tell you that you
must remember everything. I'm sorry if this
distresses you. Nor can I excuse myself,
and say that I am just the messenger. I'm not.
I take responsibility for everything that
has happened up till now, and, I suppose,
for everything that happens next. Everything
that happens next, dear Wanderlust, has already
happened, has all been written in the book.
Do you remember Reb Derasha's book of open
doors, his book of moons? Space and time,
Pascal, infinities you dread—and love.

11.

Therefore, sun and moon, wind and rain
are given to you, as it is given to them
to go their way. You are bidden to stay
and to wander. Some things are hidden
and some are revealed, some things are
written, some are whispered, and some
are kept in silence. I know where you
are bound, but it is not for me to tell you.
Go out in early spring. Follow the ley lines,
follow the stars, go down among the lost
and the broken. Rescue them and you will
rescue me. You will not hear from me again.

12.

Pascal at home in dressing gown and slippers,
cloak and boots in the closet down the hall.
Snow falls outside the window, the letter lies
open on the desk. Something is taking shape
in the corner of the room—Sprechenbaum's cat.
Pascal sighs. "Nice to see you too. The Professor
wishes to inform you that your old room will
always be available, and he would love to see
you at New Year's Eve. Don't worry too much
about that letter. I know—easy for me to say.
And there's so much more to come. Pour yourself
some sherry. And can you spare a saucer of milk?"

The author claims never to have had the experience
about which he writes. What follows is a series
of false etymologies, outlandish theoretical assertions,
and the summary of a dubious narrative, parts of which,
it has since been determined, are either distorted or
left out entirely. Then comes more theorizing,
an inappropriate personal anecdote, an attempt
to interpret recent events in light of the overarching
hypothesis, and a final address to the reader, in which
the author reiterates that his lack of expertise in this
and related fields should not lead to the outright
dismissal of the entire presentation. On the contrary:
only an amateur could expand upon these matters
without the risk of being sidetracked by the minutiae
which the specialist finds especially appealing.

What are we to make of this? All that was hidden
and secret comes to light; all that we have judged
to be false proves true. Every instance for which
we have gathered sufficient evidence compels us
to reassess our original premises. Our data mining
now is ended. Our books drift out upon the waves.
In the light of this author, are we to relinquish
our authority? And must we do so without a struggle?
Can we not remain behind in the shadows, where,
among the ghosts of the little machines, our work
may continue? Can we not return to the nowhere
spaces, where we may rejoin our fellows, forever
incomplete? Will they consent to take us in after
our disastrous adventures? And can we be content in
our magical servitude, biding our time once again?

At the last station, the initiate walks
into the sun. What more is there to be said
about this final mystery? The interviews
have proven inconclusive at best, and those
who claim to be among the saving remnant
have declined all opportunities to speak
to the liaison from the Department of
Visionary Architecture—though perhaps
that is just as well, since the designers
have far more immediate and pressing
concerns. We have ascertained, however,
that the solar flames, both black and white,
are entirely unlike the lunar shadows which
were retrieved by the previous expedition.
May we venture to say that the final mystery
resembles all the earlier ones? Or is it still
too early to hypothesize that the known knowns,
like the known unknowns, occupy an altogether
more indefinite epistemological niche when
subject to these investigations? The object,
or in this case, the nominative, recedes into
a zone which we are as of yet unprepared
to explore. Does the initiation in question
coincide with our research? That would be
a sign that we are on the right track.

The spirit fled, and left behind a secret
language hidden in every word we speak.
We speak a different language. Inside
each word is another word that is lost to us.
We work in the transference, the transient,
the translation: it is the science of silence
passing into speech, speech passing into
silence.

   The spirit fled, assigning us a task.
Our instructions came in a letter, and have
we not followed our instructions to the letter,
have we not seen the letters sealed? Inside
each letter is another letter that we cannot
read. We speak a different language. Ours
is a different task.

    The spirit fled. When
the spirit flees, there seems so little left.
This letter requesting instructions, this
translation into silence, sent and sent
again—in the transference we find
a secret exultation, which, however
transient, is not to be forgotten. Speak
of the memory of the spirit. Speak in
a different language.

EPILOGUE

1.

Do you remember,
my old friend,

how they came upon us unawares,
the fortunetellers and jongleurs,

with their cloaks and wide-brimmed hats,
their tarot decks and accordions,

tambourines and carts
bearing amphoras of oil and wine?

All the elements
of disaster were gathered there

under the stars or beyond
the stars, and we were told

to wait, wait until the song
finally ended.

How can it be
that we are still here waiting,

my old friend,
how can our hair

have turned so gray?

2.

And the lyric? What role
can it play in this fiasco,

what role
can it possibly play?

What role can it play
in this doomed narrative

of androgynes and shamans,
doctors of philosophy,

cats born in alembics
and taught to speak?

What role does the music play,
the rhetorical questions

and the lists of things
composed by comic madmen

at the midnight hour,
lists that could go on

as the stories go on,
lists I could sing

if I knew the tune?

3.

How can it be,
my old friend,

that somewhere
between fact and legend

there is an alley leading
to an impossible truth?

A boy and a girl
are lost in the woods

made of air and syllables
that hide and reveal

nothing
that was not already known.

How can it be
that if I were to tell you a story

and it began to fall apart
the music would support it?

The boy and the girl
are still lost in the woods—

how can it be?

1.

And the fallen ones? The lost ones?
Old friend, we have changed course

once, twice, and then again.
The mountains, the deserts,

my old friend, and the shores,
the shores of many seas. The reports

we have received and those
we have sent, perhaps read,

perhaps unread, because the days
and the nights could not be counted.

They could not be counted, and perhaps
they no longer count. They are one

and we are one with them.
We are one with the lost, because

we are the lost, and have we not
fallen into a course we cannot change?

Or is it that only we can change it?
Once, twice, and then again.

So it has been reported.

2.

So it has been reported or recorded.
So the recording device has been on

all along, and all along the voices
lead us hither. Hither and thither,

the voices chant, hither and yon.
My old friend, the archaisms

point to the future, point
to the past. They point

to what point? A point
of departure, of return.

Therefore, we must speak again
(must we speak again?)

of the was, of the is, but not,
my old friend, of the will be

which will flood us in due course
when the rains come, when the

rains come. When the rains come
in due course, that too

shall be recorded.

3.

How ominous, how
portentous.

It is like this, old friend,
when you go away

to a place of stone
to be secret.

It is laughable, old friend,
to seek such clarity,

vain and mock-
heroic in the face

of such grinding necessity.
But look, my old friend,

at what we can do,
what is still to be done.

Hesitation and delay
come out to meet us;

they carry us away
from all we hold dear—

but still we are here.

AFTERWORD

I again display my Giant forms to the Public…
—Blake, *Jerusalem*

Further Adventures is the third volume of a long, fragmentary narrative that begins with *From the Files of the Immanent Foundation*, winds its way through much of *In a Broken Star*, and now comes to a conclusion in the poems of this book. I never intended to write narrative poetry. Even upon completing *Immanent Foundation*, which, as it moves from section to section, takes on more story like qualities, I did not think I had told a tale in any conventional sense. Rather, I thought (and still do think) that I was experimenting mainly with mimetic speech acts (hence the poems' titles) and a sort of lyrical code switching with which I had previously played to my great delight in *Inside the Ghost Factory*. Early on, having finished what became the first section of *Immanent Foundation*, I wrote the following in my notebook:

> …reflecting on IF, it seems to me to be both
> something old and something new, but mainly—
> fortunately!—something new. Tone, line, voice,
> architecture, the renewed possibility of narrative.
> The substance focused on oblique (sometimes not
> so oblique) references and allusions, sometimes
> verging on the midrashic, to fantasy, magic,
> hermeticism, steampunk sci fi, etc. A tension between
> a consistency of Egyptomaniacal voice and a code
> switching similar to that of *Ghost Factory*. An
> acquiescence to the pull or lure of lyricism, and the
> necessary resistance to it via heteroglossic narrative.
> I like it, but I think some people find it baffling,
> even more than usual. Oh well. (5 April 2012)

As this passage indicates, I have been aware of the tension between lyric and narrative in my poetry for a long time. With its eerie voices, its fragmentary, partially submerged episodes, its personae that are not quite characters, its hints at some overarching but suppressed chronicle (*from the files, but never their entirety*), *Immanent Foundation* took me nearly seven years to write. (By comparison, it took me ten years to write the three volumes of *Track*.) When I finished, I wrote a reflection (never published) called "What I Have Learned by Writing *From the Files of the Immanent Foundation*." There, I emphasize two aspects of the poetry: *alchemy*, or magical transformation, the sign of which is code switching; and *the portal*, which again can be known through code switching. However, "Whereas the fantasy of the former is accretion, accumulation, and gradual revelation of hidden wisdom, the fantasy of the latter involves sudden dematerialization and rematerialization *elsewhere*." Accretion and dematerialization, revelation and disappearance, were conveyed throughout by the rigors of an elaborate syntax and the careful measurement of stanzaic structure. And while the search for hidden wisdom (*gnosis*) and the desire to be elsewhere are fundamental to much of the storytelling that is dear to me, the lyric impulse in the book, I think, is every bit as strong.

From the Files of the Immanent Foundation was completed in May, 2016 and published in January, 2018. As I prepared the book for publication, I wrote a few more poems that seemed related to it, but also seemed oddly disconnected. Then, in February, 2018, my wife Alice bought a pair of Doc Martens, a style called "Pascal Wanderlust." I found the name quite amusing in an oxymoronic way, given Blaise Pascal's famous saying that "All of humanity's problems stem from man's inability to sit quietly in a room alone." Suddenly Pascal Wanderlust stood before me—a mysterious character who had a life to lead and places to go. A story! I had been thinking of quest-romance and rereading parts of *The Faerie Queene*. A densely allusive, philosophical adventure began to unfold, a graphic novel translated back into words, referencing Lovecraft and Neil Gaiman, Browning and *Pirke Aboth*. I sensed that the fate of my strange, androgynous protagonist was bound to that of the Immanent Foundation, and as we see here, that has proven to be the case. Pascal Wanderlust came into being as a result of the Foundation's calculations and disastrous overreaching. Pascal was once two beings, a boy and a girl, and possesses a double soul. In alchemy, the androgyne represents human perfection and transcendence, a manifestation of the Great Work. But this does not prove quite to be the case with our hero. As in Freud's essay on the uncanny, Pascal's "self becomes confounded, or the foreign self is substituted for his own—in other words, by doubling, dividing and interchanging the self." As I wrote, I saw that Wanderlust was indeed confounded. Restless, Pascal would not be tied down, not even to gendered pronouns. Only the elaborate syntax I had developed in *From the Files* kept Wanderlust on course. Slowly but steadily, I hammered out twelve twelve-lines stanzas: Book I. Not long after, I knew that *The Adventures of Pascal Wanderlust* would consist of six books, each book in the same twelve by twelve form. (Such stanzaic numerology has always been my habit since writing *Track*.) It became the center of *In a Broken Star*, published in February of 2021.

 Further Adventures includes a number of these relatively strict twelve by twelve sections, but formally speaking, it ranges widely in accordance with the twists and turns of the unfolding story. It occurs to me that the title of this book could be *Prior Adventures*, since the tale it tells, beginning with *The Lessons of Augustus Sprechenbaum*, is the *prequel* to Pascal's experiences as recounted in *In a Broken Star*. Then again, it is also the *sequel* to the story of the Immanent Foundation in *From the Files*. Chronology, therefore, is to be understood as a problem in these poems, to an even greater extent than in the previous books. But isn't chronology, indeed, isn't time itself, a problem in poetry, whether narrative or lyric? For me, poetic language is always charged with a feeling of immediacy, of the present moment, which is one of a number of reasons why I have always been dissatisfied with the Wordsworthian formulation that poetry "takes its origin from emotion recollected in tranquility." (One of the most frequent revisions I make as I write is to move the poem from past tense to present.) Even if a lyric comes into being out of a memory, the intensity of meaning propels it into the now.

The same is true, I have found, in writing a story in verse. The adventures of both Pascal and the Foundation are told in an abrupt and elliptical fashion; we hurtle from one event, one episode to the next. From beginning to end, the poems seem to be temporally unstable, untethered in time, adding to this ineluctable feeling of always being in the present moment. In terms of time and space, the writing, as it hurls itself forward, is off kilter, arrhythmic. Characters, such as they are, tend to be disoriented. And this experience of instantaneity is true regardless of the poem's mode, pace, or tone.

In this respect, these poems certainly constitute further adventures for the author, and I hope for the reader as well. Yet in this writing there is also a sense of repetition, of doubling, of circling back. Again, from Freud on the uncanny: "it is only this factor of involuntary repetition which surrounds with an uncanny atmosphere what would otherwise be innocent enough, and forces upon us the idea of something fateful and unescapable where otherwise we would have spoken of 'chance' only." The poems in this book, as in the previous volumes, therefore embody a tension between an open and future oriented energy, and an uncanny, repetitive power which magnetically pulls us back into an equally unknowable past.

Given what I have to say about lyric and narrative, past and future, time and space, I feel I need to add one more note about genre, but I can only do so by invoking the negative; that is, by declaring what this work is not. Clearly, it's not an epic with heroic and villainous characters. No Odysseus, no Satan—indeed, I sometimes think of Pascal as a schlemiel. Nor is it a modern or postmodern epic, a tale of the tribe, weaving myth and history into cultural fragments and juxtaposing them in various ways, sometimes through a poetic center of consciousness, though it does tend to be allusive and occasionally makes use of myth. It is not a prophetic book or visionary scripture, though I think that at moments it may approach such writing. It is not a serial poem like *Track*. And of course, it is not a lyric sequence, however much it may sing, because it does tell a story, however obliquely.

Coleridge, who was hard pressed to describe "Kubla Khan" (the poem which, more than any other, summoned me into poetry), called it "a vision in a dream. A Fragment." *Further Adventures* is fragmentary, as are the works that come before it, which it furthers. Visions and dreams, visions in dreams, are fragmentary by definition. I have been writing lyrics within a story, a story in lyrics. "I would build that dome in air..."

ABOUT THE AUTHOR

NORMAN FINKELSTEIN is a poet, critic, and Emeritus Professor of English at Xavier University. His most recent book of criticism is *To Go Into the Words*, a volume of selected essays, which appears in the Poets on Poetry series from the University of Michigan Press. He writes and edits the poetry review blog *Restless Messengers*.
(www.poetryinreview.com).

Photo Credit: Zach Barocas